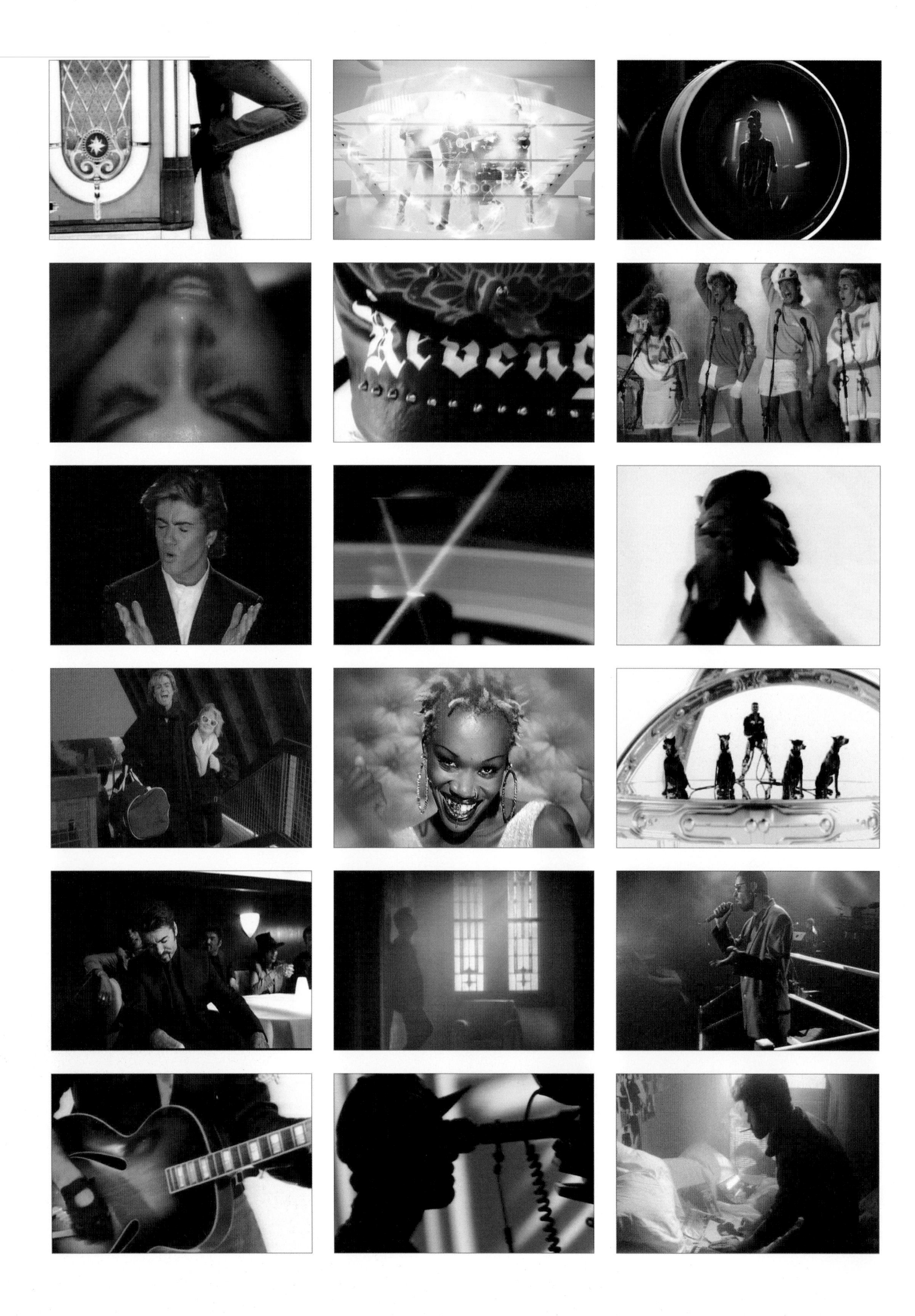

1999

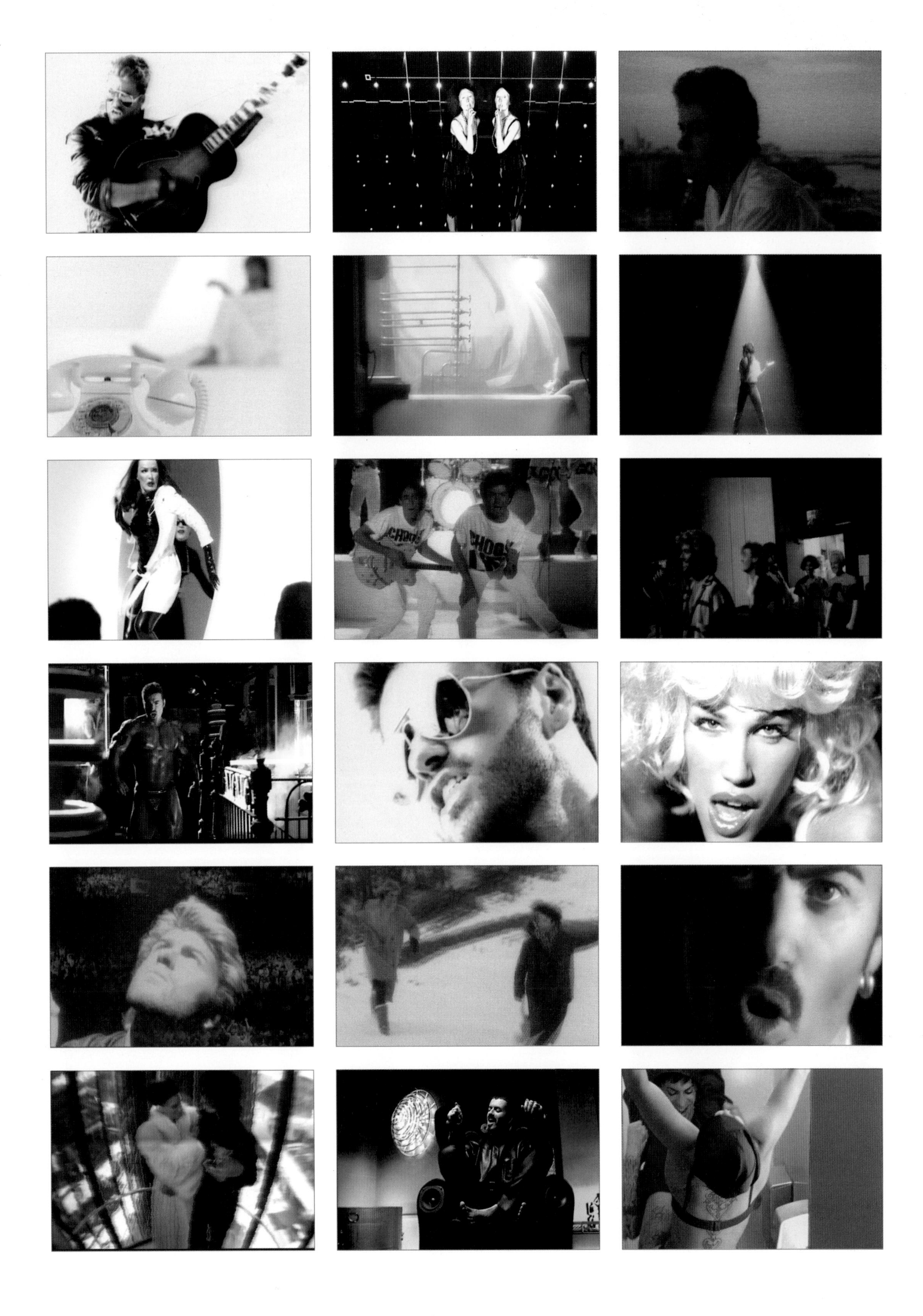

GEORGE MICHAEL TWENTY FIVE

FOR LIVING

First published by Faber Music Ltd in 2007
3 Queen Square, London WC1N 3AU

Re-Engravings : Cotswold Music Typesetting.
New Arrangements : Richard Harris.
Editor : Lucy Holliday.
Cover Design : George Michael & Simon Halfon.
Cover Photography : Andrew Macpherson.

Printed in England by Caligraving Ltd.

The text paper used in this publication is a virgin fibre product
that is manufactured in the UK to ISO 14001 standards.
The wood fibre used is only sourced from managed forests using
sustainable forestry principles. This paper is 100% recyclable

ISBN10: 0-571-52994-1
EAN13: 978-0-571-52994-0

To buy Faber Music publications or to find out about the full range of titles available,
please contact your local music retailer or Faber Music sales enquiries:

Faber Music Ltd, Burnt Mill, Elizabeth Way, Harlow, CM20 2HX England.
tel:+44(0)1279 82 89 82 fax:+44(0)1279 82 89 83
sales@fabermusic.com fabermusic.com.

EVERYTHING SHE WANTS

Words and Music by George Michael

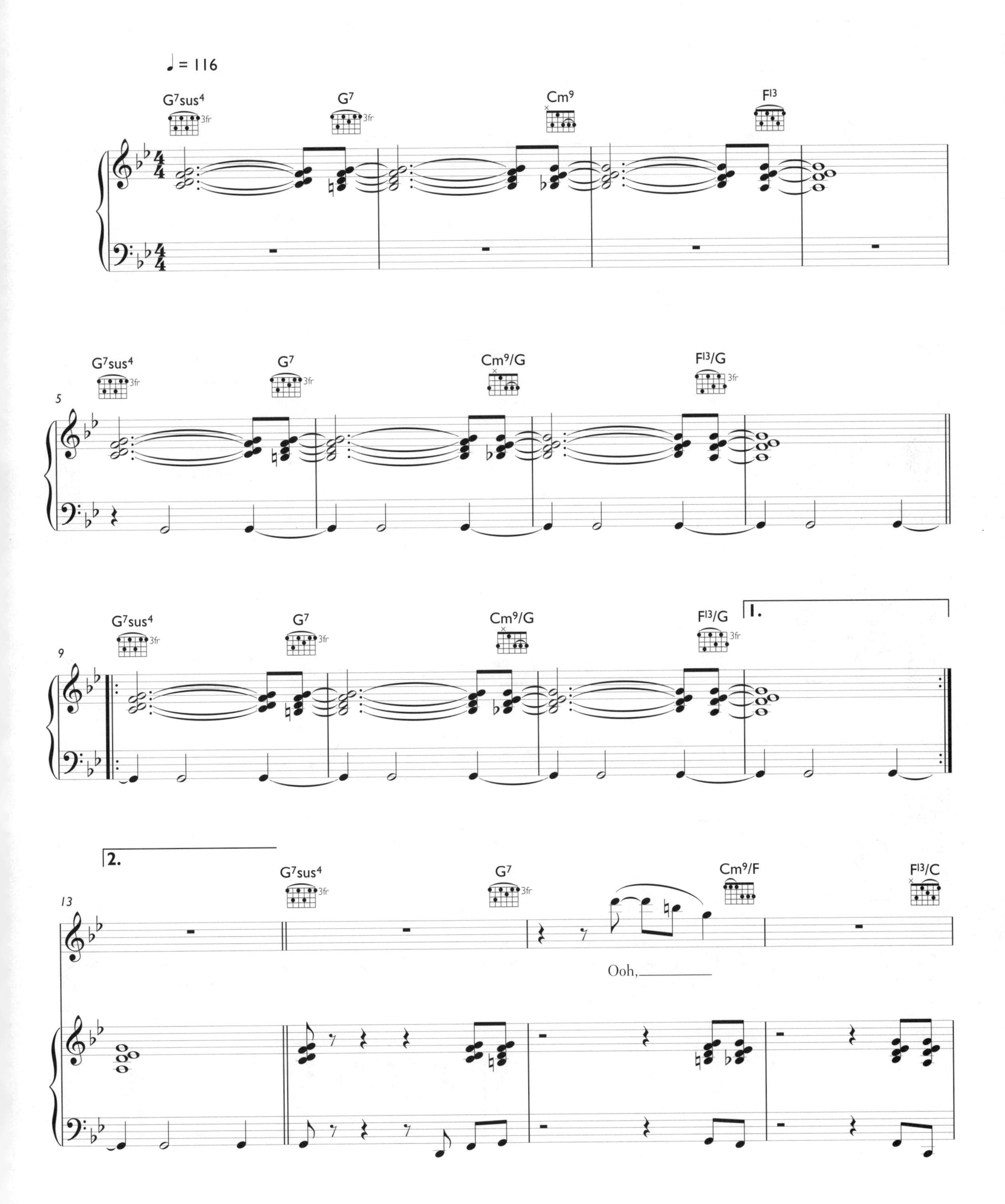

G7sus4
G7
Cm9/F
F13/C
oh yeah.
G
Cm7
1. Some-bo-dy told me, boy, ev-'ry-thing she wants is
Cm7/F
ev-'ry-thing she sees. I guess I must have loved you be-cause I said you were the per-fect girl
G7sus4
G7
for me, ba-by. And now we're six months old-er and ev-'ry-thing you want and
3fr

F13
G7
3fr
Cm7
3fr
33
ev - 'ry-thing you see
is out of reach, not
good e - nough
I don't know what the hell
you want
Cm7/F
G7sus4
3fr
G7
Cm7
3fr
37
from me, oh.
Ah,
oh,
oh,
ah,
ah,
do, do, do,
F13
G7sus4
3fr
G7
3fr
Cm7
3fr
41
la, la, la, la, la.
Ah,
oh,
oh,
ah,
ah,
do, do, do,
F13
Cm7
3fr
D13
4fr
Dm7/F
Gm7
3fr
45
la, la, la, la, la.
Some - bo - dy
tell
me

Cm7
Dm7/F
D7/F♯
Gm7
3fr
49
(won't you tell me), why I work so hard for you (work
53
G7sus4
G7
to give you mo- ney).
57
F13
1.
61
2. Some peo-ple work for a liv - ing, some peo-ple work for fun, girl

F13
G7sus4
3fr
G7
3fr
Cm7
3fr
65
I just work for you. They told me marr-iage was a give and take, well you've shown me you can take you've got some
Cm7/F
G7sus4
3fr
G7
3fr
Cm7
3fr
69
giv-ing to do. And now you tell me that you're hav-ing my ba - by, I'll tell you that I'm hap-py if you
F13
G7sus4
3fr
G7
3fr
Cm7
3fr
73
want me to. But one step fur-ther and my back will break, if my best is - n't good e-nough then how
Cm7/F
G7sus4
3fr
G7
3fr
Cm7
3fr
77
can it be good e-nough for two? Ah, oh, oh, ah, ah, I can't work

C13
G7sus4
2.
F13
Gm
81
— a-ny hard-er than I do Ah oh
Oh.
Cm7
Gm7
85
Why do I do the things I do?
I'd tell you if I knew.
Cm7
F13
Cm7
D13
89
My God
I don't ev-en think that I love you,
Dm7/F
Gm7
Cm7
Dm7/F
93
(won't you tell me),

97
D7/F♯
Gm7
Gm
F
Gm
(give you mo-ney, work to give you mo - ney)...
vocal ad lib.
101
F
Gm
Dm
C
Dm
D7
Gm7
Gm
F
Gm
105
F
Gm
Dm
C
Dm
D7sus4
D7
Cm7
How could you set-tle for a
109
Dm7
Gm7
C7
E♭maj7
boy like me when all I could see was the end of the week? All the things we sign and the things

Am7 D7 Gm F Gm
113
we buy ain't gon-na keep us to-geth-er it's just a mat-ter of time My sit-u-a-
F Gm Dm C Dm D7 Gm7 Gm F Gm
117
-tion ne-ver chan-ges, walk-ing in and out of that door like a strang-
F Gm Dm C Dm D7 Cm7
121
-er for the wa-ges I give you all, you say you want more
Dm7 Gm7 C7 E♭maj7
125
And all I could see was the end of the week. All the things we sign and the things

Am7
D7
G7sus4
129
we buy ain't gon-na keep us to-ge-ther, girl, it's just a mat-ter of time.
G7
Cm7
F13
G7sus4
133
La, la, la, la. Ah, oh,
G7
Cm7
F13
Cm7
D13
137
oh, ah, ah, do, do, do, la, la, la, la, la.
Dm7/F
Gm7
Cm7
Dm7/F
141
Some - bo - dy tell me, (won't you tell me) why I work

D7/F♯
Gm7
3fr
145
so hard for you,
(oh, to give you mo - ney).

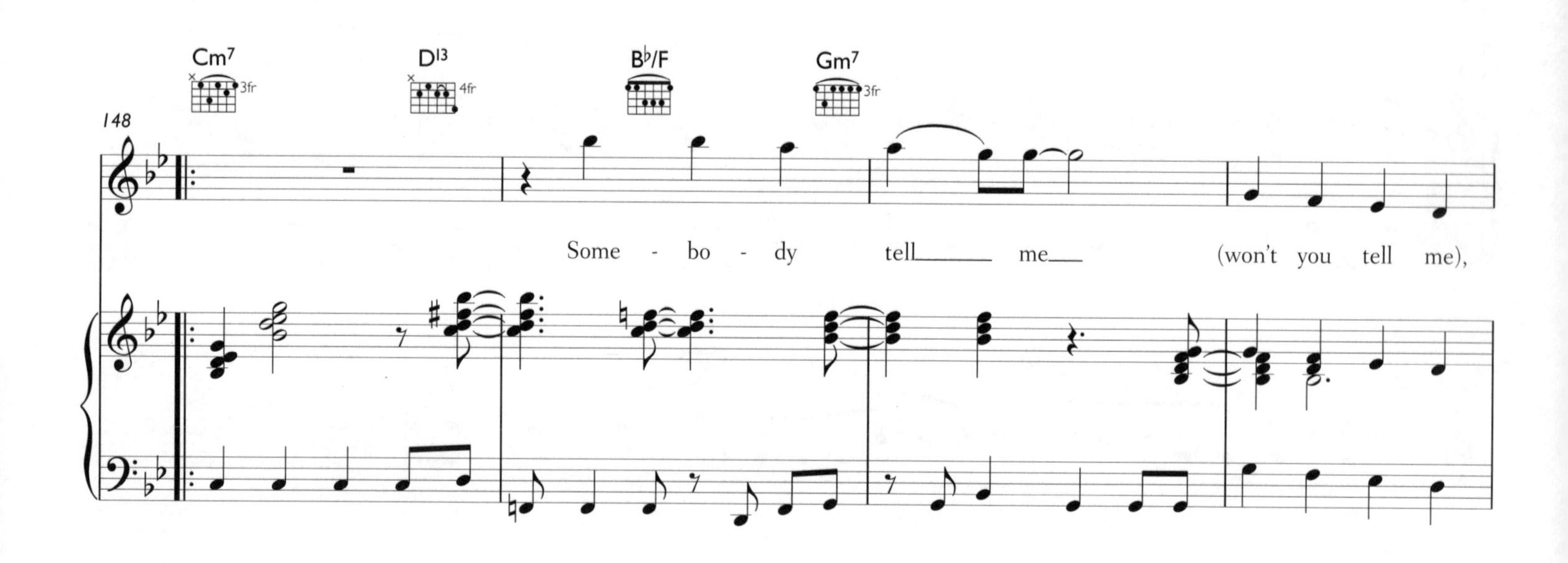
Cm7
3fr
D13
4fr
B♭/F
Gm7
3fr
148
Some - bo - dy tell me
(won't you tell me),

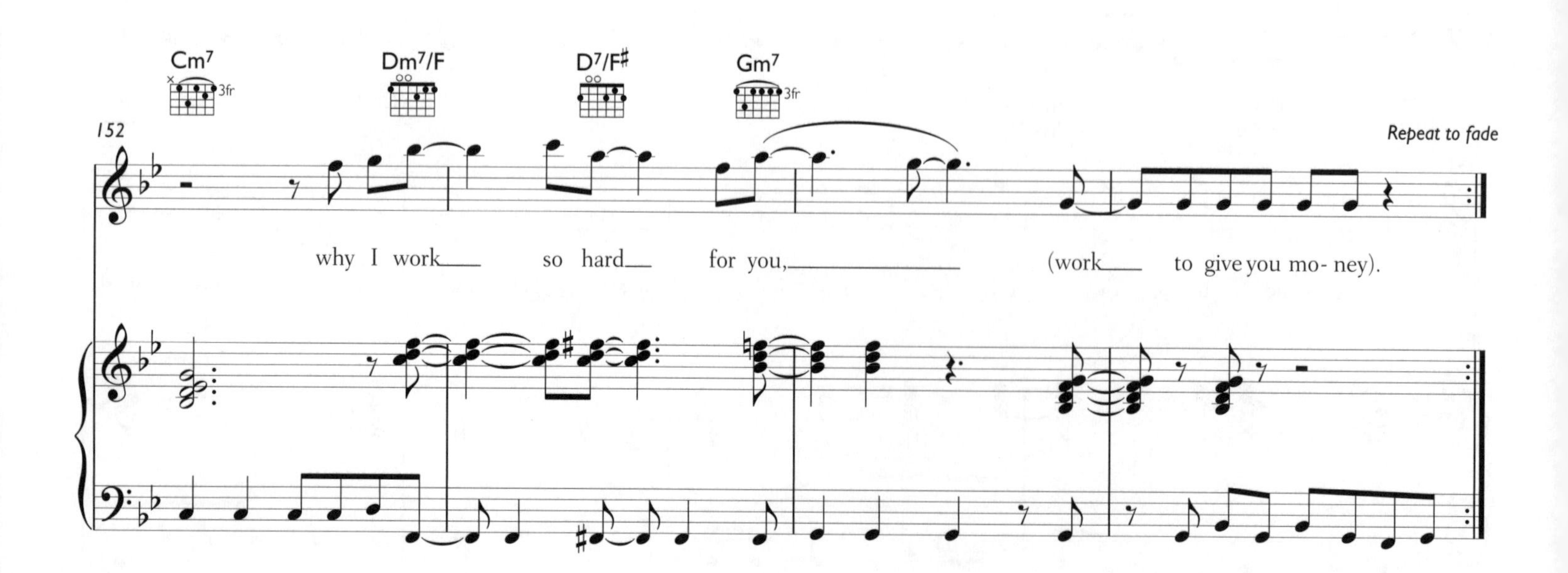
Cm7
3fr
Dm7/F
D7/F♯
Gm7
3fr
152
Repeat to fade
why I work so hard for you,
(work to give you mo - ney).

WAKE ME UP BEFORE YOU GO-GO

Words and Music by George Michael

Em
F
Em
A11
Dm
13
some - thing ain't right, my best friend told me what you did last night, left me sleep - ing
I'm your fool, it makes me cra - zy when you act so cruel, come on ba - by,
move in tight, we'll go danc - ing to - mor - row night. It's cold out there but it's
Em
F
G
N.C.
17
in my bed. I was dream - ing but I should have been with you in - stead.
let's not fight, we'll go danc - ing, ev - 'ry - thing will be al - right.
warm in bed, they can dance, we'll stay home in - stead.
Wake me up
C
Dm
C
21
before you go go, don't leave me hang - ing on like a yo - yo. Wake me up
Dm
25
before you go go, I don't wan - na miss it when you hit that high.

28
C
Dm
Wake me up before you go go 'cause I'm not plan - ning on go - ing so -
32
C
C7/E
Dm
- lo. Wake me up be - fore you go go, take me danc - ing to - night.
1.2.
36
C
F/C
C
C7
I wan-na hit that high,
41
F/C
C
yeah yeah. 2. You put the
3.
C
N.C.
D.𝄋 and fade
Wake me up

FREEDOM

Words and Music by George Michael

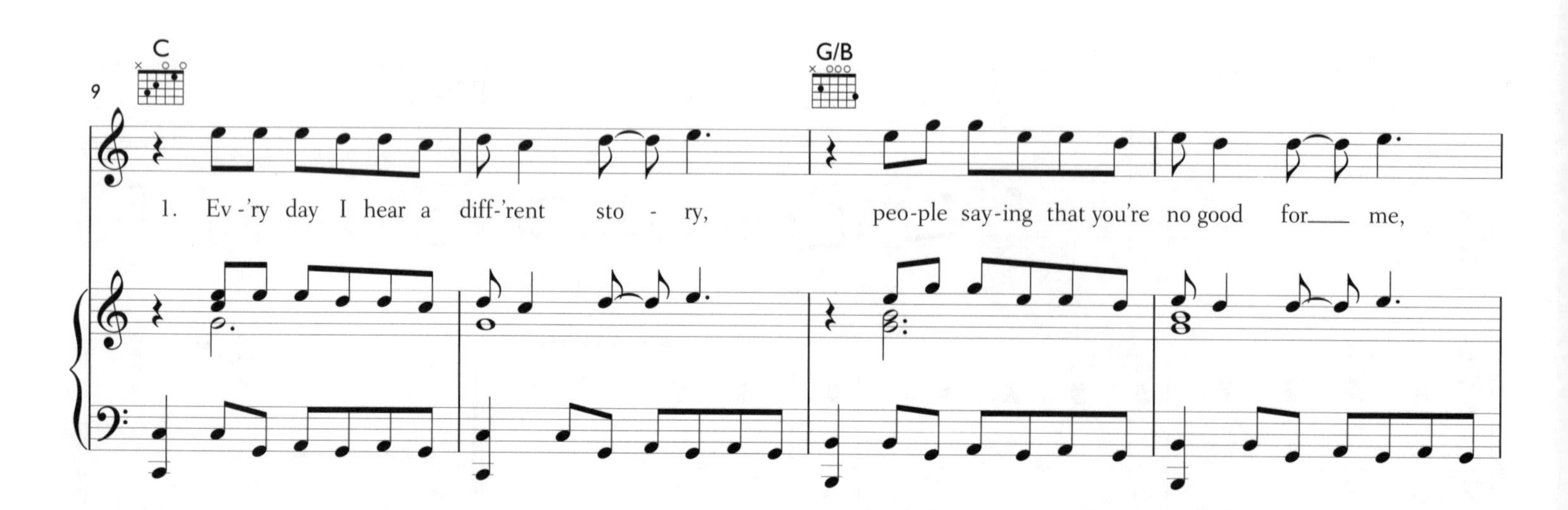

Dm
C
G/B
Am
G
13
3
saw your lov - er with a - no-ther and she's mak - ing a fool of you, oh.
17
If you loved me, ba - by you would de - ny it, but you laugh and tell me I should try it,
F
21
tell me I'm a ba - by and I don't un - der-stand. But you know that I'll for-give
26
you just this once, twice, for - ev - er, 'cos ba - by you could drag me to

G
C
G/B
Am
Am/G
Fmaj7
30
hell and back just as long as we're to-geth - er, and you do.
G
C
C/E
F
Dm
34
I don't want your free - dom, I don't want to
C/G
G
C
C/E
F
Dm
C/E
F
38
play a-round, I don't want no - bo - dy ba - by, part - time love just
C/G
G
C
C/E
B♭/F
Dm7
42
brings me down I don't need your free - - dom,
2° want

G
N.C.
C
C/E
F
46
girl all I want right now is you.
Do do do,
50
woah, yeah.
Do do do do do do
do do do do do do.
54
1.
G/B
2. Like a pri-son-er who has his own key
but I can't es-cape un-
58
Dm
-til you love me, I just go from day to day know-ing all a-bout the

Am G C G/B
62
oth - er boys. You take my hand and tell me I'm a fool to give you all that I do
Dm C G/B Am G
66
I bet you some-day ba - by some-one says the same to you. But you
2.
C G/B Dm
71
Hurt-ing me ba - by,
C G/B Am G C
76
hurt-ing me ba - by...
Do do do do do do do,

G/B
Dm
80
do do do do do do do,
do do do do do do do,
do do do do do do do,
hurt-ing me ba - by,
C
G/B
Am
G
F
G
84
hurt-ing me ba - by...
But you know that I'll for- give you just this
C
G/B
Am
G
F
G
89
once, twice, for - ev - er 'cos ba - by you could drag me to hell and back just as long
C
G/B
Am
Am/G
Fmaj7
G
93
as we're to - ge - ther and you do, oh.

C
C/E
F
Dm
C/G
G
97
I don't want your free - dom I don't need to play a - round,
2° want
C
C/E
F
Dm
C/E
C/G
G
101
I don't want no - bo - dy ba - by, part - time love just brings me down.
C
C/E
Fsus4
F
Dm7
C/G
G
105
I don't want your, I don't want your, I don't want your, I don't want your,
C
C/E
Fsus4
F
Dm7
C/G
G
C
C/E
109
I don't want your, I don't want your...

B♭/F
F
Dm7
C/G
G
C
C/E
Fsus4
F
Gsus4
G
3fr
(to fade)
G7

FAITH

Words and Music by George Michael

13
E
be-fore I give my heart a-way, and I know all the games you play
you mean ev-'ry word you say, can't help but think of yes-ter-day
17
B
E
be-cause I played them too. Oh but I need some-time-
and an-other who tied me down to lov-er boy rules. 2,3. Be-fore this riv-
21
B
E
off from that e-mo-tion, time to pick my heart
-er be-comes an o-cean, be-fore you throw my heart
25
B
E
up off the floor. Oh when that love comes down
back on the floor. Oh baby I re-con-sid-

B
G♯m
4fr
C♯m
4fr
— with - out de - vo - tion, well it takes a strong — man ba -
- er my fool - ish — no - tion, well I need some - one — to hold
F♯
N.C.
B
(3° 𝄐)
- by but I'm show-ing you — the door. Be-cause I've got to have faith,
— me but I'll wait for some - thing more. Yes I've got to have faith,
I've got to have faith, — be-cause I've got to have faith, faith, — faith,
1.
2.
3.
N.C.
I've got to have faith, a' faith, — a' faith. 2. Ba -

TOO FUNKY

Words and Music by George Michael

Dm G/D Am/D G/D Dm G/D Am/D G/D
15
I've got to get in - side of you.
I've watched your fin-gers work-ing o - ver - time,
I've watched your drink-ing and I take my_ time,
Dm G/D Am/D G/D Dm G/D
19
I've got to think-ing that they should be_ mine.
I watch you sink-ing all of that cheap red_ wine._
I'd love
I've got
to see you nak - ed ba-
Am/D G/D Dm G/D Am/D G/D
22
- by, I'd like to think_ that some - time may - be to - night
if that's al - right.
my goal's in sight.
Yeah.
1.
Dm G/D Am/D G/D Dm G/D
25
(Solo keyboard)

Am/D
G/D
Dm
2.
1.
Baby, baby, baby why do you do this to me?
Won't let you go,
you're such a, you're such a,
I've got to know.
Gon-na be the kind of lov-er that you nev-er had. Hey, you're just too funk-y.

Dm
G/D
Am/D
41
You're ne - ver gon - na have an - oth - er lov - er in your bed.
You're just too funk - y for me.
43
(Solo keyboard)
46
Ev - 'ry - bo - dy wants a lov - er like that.
(Would you like me to seduce you? Is that what you're trying to tell me?)
50
Ev - 'ry - bo - dy wants a lov - er like that.
(Ev'rybody, ev'rybody) yeah yeah.

("Would you stop playing with that radio of yours? I'm trying to get to sleep!")

FASTLOVE

Words and Music by Patrice Rushen, Fred Washington,
Terri McFaddin and George Michael

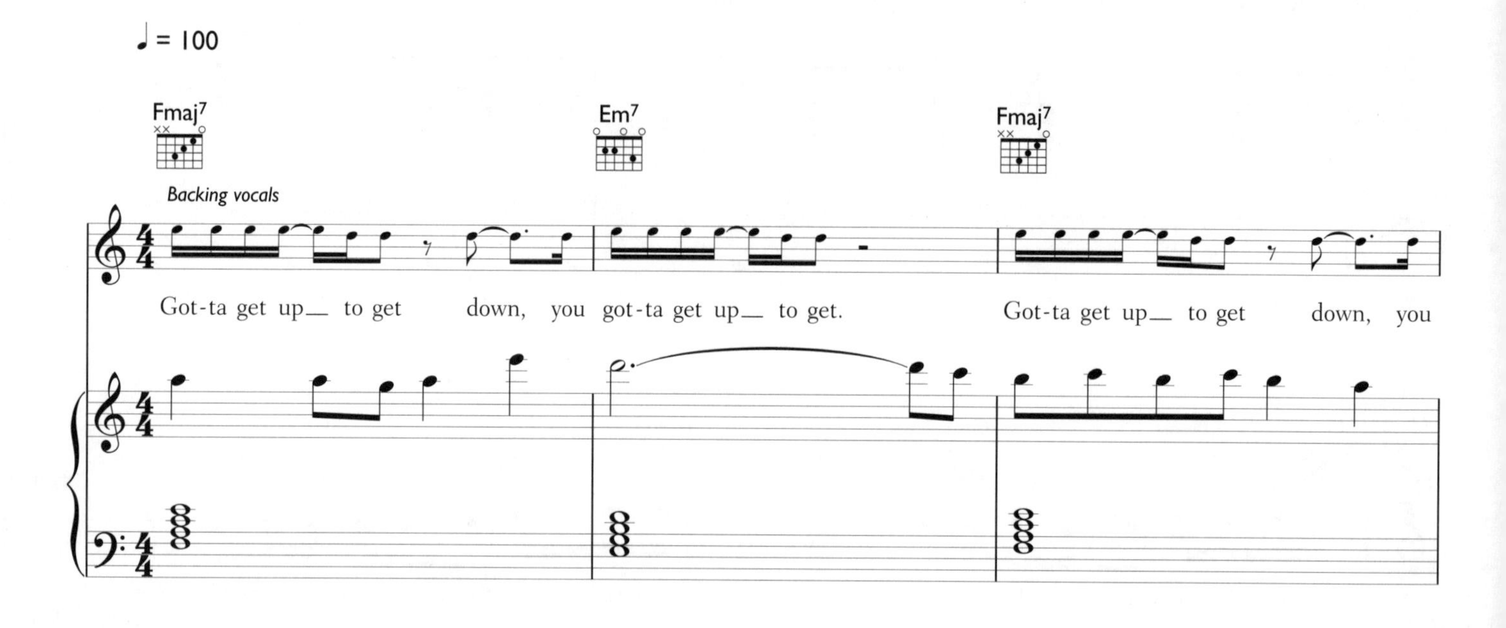

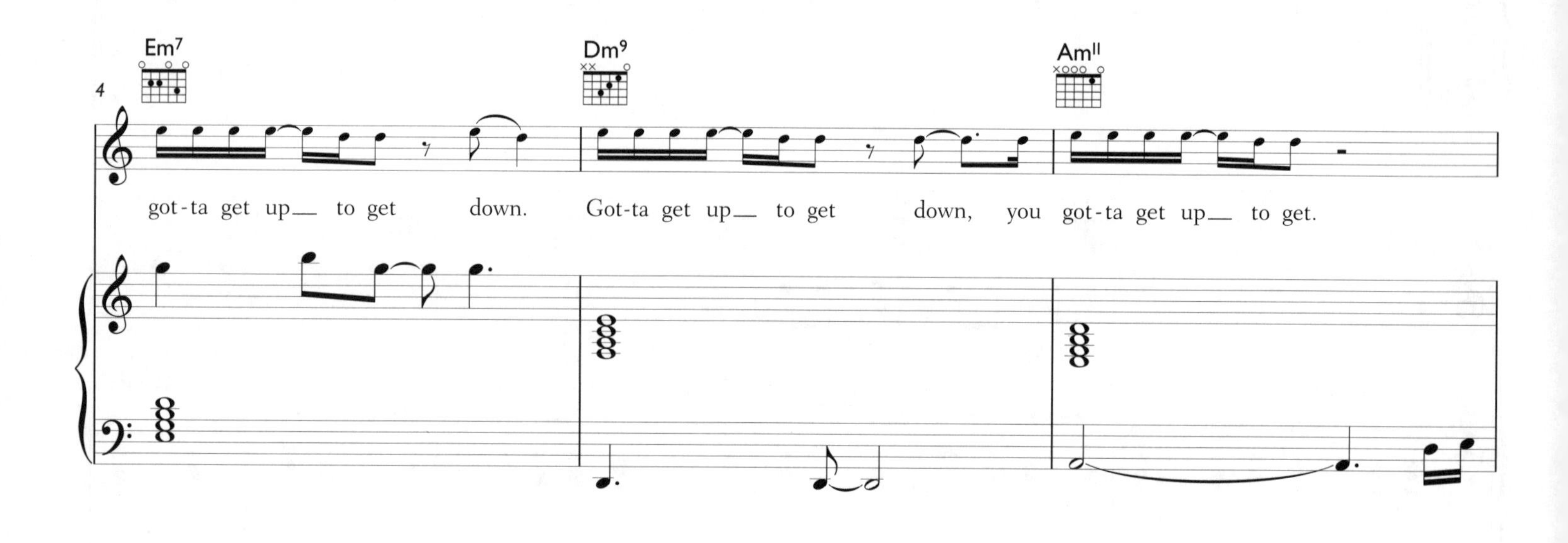

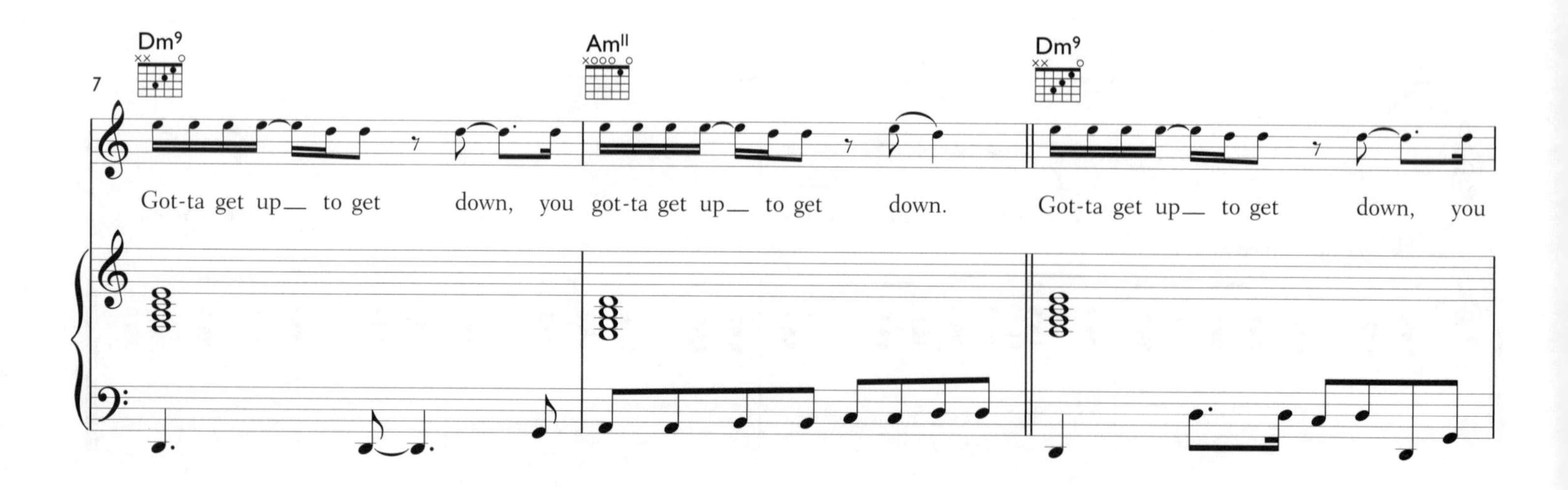

Am11
Dm9
Am11
10
got-ta get up — to get down. You got-ta get up — to get down, you got-ta get up — to get down.
Dm9
Am11
Dm9
13
Got-ta get up — to get down, you got-ta get up — to get down. You got-ta get up — to get down, you
Am11
Dm9
Am11
16
got-ta get up — to get down. 1. Look - ing for — some e - du - ca - tion,
2. - ing for — some af - fir - ma - tion,
Dm9
Am11
Dm9
19
made my way in - to the night. — All — that bull - shit con -
made my way in - to the sun. — My friends got their la - dies, they're

Am11
Dm9
Am11
22
- ver - sa - tion, ba - by can't you read the signs?
all hav-ing ba - bies, but I just want to have some fun.
Dm9
Am11
Dm9
25
I won't bore you with the de - tail ba - by, I don't e - ven want to waste your time.
I won't bore you with the de - tail ba - by, got-ta get there in your own sweet time.
Let's just say that may - be
Am11
Dm9
Am11
Dm9
28
you could help to ease my mind. Ba - by I ain't Mis - ter Right.
Am11
Am7
Fmaj7
Am7
32
But if you're look-ing for fast love, if that's love in your eyes. It's

Dm9
Am7
Fmaj7
Em7
36
more than in love, had some bad luck, so fast love is all that I've got on
Dm9
Am11
Dm9
Am11
40
Vocals ad lib.
my mind.
Instrumental ad lib.
Dm9
Am11
Dm9
1.
Am11
45
2. Look -
2.
Am11
Dm9
Am11
49
Backing vocals (lead vocal ad lib.)
Got-ta get up to get down, you got-ta get up to get down. You

Dm9
Am11
N.C.
52
got - ta get up to get down, you got - ta get up to get down. You
Drum break
55
Am7
Fmaj9
G6
Em7
58
In the ab - sence of se - cu - ri - ty
I made my way in - to the night.
61
Stu - pid Cu - pid keeps on call - ing me,

Am7
Fmaj9
G6
Em7
64
well I see lov-ing in his eyes.
I miss my ba - by,
oh yeah!
67
I miss my ba - by,
to - night.
So why don't we make
70
a lit-tle room in my B M W babe?
Search-ing for some peace of mind.
73
Hey! I'll help you find it.
I do be - lieve that we are prac - tis - ing the same re - li - gion.

Am7
Fmaj9
G6
Em7
76
Oh! You real-ly ought to get up now.
79
That's right.
Oh! You real-ly ought to get up.
Backing vocals (lead vocal ad lib.)
Got-ta get up to get down, you
83
got-ta get up to get down. You got-ta get up to get down, you got-ta get up to get down. You
Am9
86
Play x4
got-ta get up to get down, you got-ta get up to get down. (You)

FREEDOM '90

Words and Music by George Michael

F
C
'cause I would real - ly, real - ly love to stick a-round, oh
yeah.
B♭
F
C
gliss.
B♭
F
C
G
1. Hea-ven knows I was just a
2. Hea-ven knows we sure had some

F
F/C
C
22
echo
young boy, did - n't know what I want - ed to be
fun boy, what a kick, just a bud - dy and me
(did - n't know what I want - ed to be).
(what a kick, just a bud - dy and me).
F/C
C
G
24
I was ev - 'ry lit - tle hun - gry school - girl's pride
We had ev - 'ry big shot good time band on the run
F
F/C
C
26
echo
and joy and I guess it was e - nough for me.
boy, we were liv - ing in a fan - ta - sy.
(And I guess it was e - nough for me.)
(We were liv - ing in a fan - ta - sy.)
F/C
C
G
28
To win the race, a pret - ti - er face, brand
We won the race, got out - ta the place, went

F
F/C
C
echo
(rock and roll T. V.)
(boys at M. T. V.)
new clothes and a big fat place on your rock and roll T. V.
back home got a brand new face for the boys at M. T. V.
F/C
C
G
But to - day, the way you play the game is not the same,
But to - day, the way I play the game has got to change,
F
C
no way, think I'm gon - na get me some hap - py.
oh yeah, now I'm gon - na get me some hap - py.
Cm
3fr
gliss.
I think there's some - thing you should know,
I think there's some - thing you should know,

Cm(maj7)
3fr
Cm7
3fr
I think it's time I told you so, there's some-thing deep in-side of me,
I think it's time I stopped the show, there's some-thing deep in-side of me,
Cm6
4fr
Cm
3fr
there's some-one else I've got to be. Take back your pic-ture in the frame,
there's some-one I for-got to be. Take back your pic-ture in the frame,
Cm(maj7)
3fr
Cm7
3fr
take back your "Sing-ing In The Rain". Just hope you'll un-der-stand. Some-
don't think that I'll be back a-gain. Just hope you'll un-der-stand. Some-
G
C
-times the clothes do not make the man.
-times the clothes do not make the man.
All we have to do

B♭
F
C
46
now is to take these lies and make them true some - how.
49
B♭
F
All we have to see is that I don't be-long to you and you
C
B♭
52
don't be - long to me, yeah, yeah. (Free - dom!)
(Free - dom!)
I won't let you down, I will not give you up,
F
C
55
(Free - dom!)
You've got to give for what you take.
got to have some faith in the sound. It's the one good thing that I've

B♭
57
(Free - dom!)
got, I won't let you down,
(Free - dom!)
so please don't give me up,
F
C
59
(Free - dom!)
You've got to give for what you take.
'cause I would real - ly, real - ly love to stick a-round.
Cm
Cm6
Cm
61
Cm6
(Vocal 2°)
Cm
64
Well it looks like the road to hea - ven, but it feels

Cm(maj7)
3fr
66
Cm7
3fr
like the road to hell.
But I know which side my bread was but - tered, I
Cm6
4fr
68
Cm
3fr
took the knife as well.
Pos - ing for a - no - ther pic - ture ev -
Cm(maj7)
3fr
70
Cm7
3fr
- 'ry - bo - dy's got to sell,
but when you shake your ass they no - tice fast
Cm6
4fr
72
Cm
3fr
(that's what you get)
some mis - takes were built to last.
That's what you get,
that's

Cm(maj7)
3fr
Cm7
3fr
74
(I say that's what you get)
(That's
what you get,
I say that's what you get for chang - ing your mind.
Cm6
4fr
Cm
3fr
76
what you get for chang - ing your mind.)
That's what you get
(that's
Cm(maj7)
3fr
Cm7
3fr
78
what you get,)
and af - ter all this time
I just hope you'll un - der - stand. Some -
G
C
B♭
80
- times the clothes do not make the man. All we have to do now is to

F
C
83
take these lies___ and make them true___ (some - how). All we have to see___
B♭
F
C
86
is that I don't be - long_ to you___ and you don't be - long_ to me,___ yeah, yeah._
B♭
F
89
Free - dom! Oh,___ free - dom!___ My free - dom!___ You've got to
C
B♭
92
give for what you take.___ Free - dom! Hold on___ to my free - dom!___ My

F
C
95
free - dom!
You've got to give for what you, give for what you, give for what
97
B♭
F
you take.
Yeah, you've got to
100
C
C
give for what you, give for what you take. It may not be what you want from me,
102
B♭
F
C
Repeat to fade
that's the way it's got to be, lose the face now, got to give, got to give, got to give. It

SPINNING THE WHEEL

Words and Music by George Michael and Johnny Douglas

G#7
C#m
11
14
G#7
17
C#m
1.Five o' clock in the morn - ing, you ain't home, I can't help think-ing that's
2.Six o' clock in the morn - ing, you ain't phoned, I can't help think-ing that's
19
G#7
C#m
strange, yeah yeah. Ba - by, I just want you to know
strange, yeah yeah. It seems that ev-'ry-bo-dy takes their chan-ces

G#7
I won't go through it a - gain, yeah yeah. Those clouds are clos - ing in,
these days, oh yeah. We're stand - ing in the rain,
Amaj7
G#m7
Amaj7
and I will not ac - cept this as a part of my life. I will not live
G#m7
Amaj7
in fear of what may be, and the les -

G♯m7
Amaj7
30
- sons I have learned with you, I would ra - ther be a- lone than watch you
G♯11
A♯m
32
spin - ning that wheel for me. You've got a thing a - bout dan - ger, ain't you
A
B
A♯m
34
get-ting what you want from me? You've got a thing a - bout stran - gers ba - by,
A
B
A♯m
36
that's what we used to be. You've got a thing a - bout dan - ger ba - by,

A
B
A♯m
38
I guess the hun - gry just can't see.
A
B
C♯m
40
1.
One of these days you're gon-na bring some home to me.
G♯7
C♯m
43
G♯7
47
2.
Amaj7
How can

G#m7
Amaj7
G#m7
50
you love me
when you are play - ing with my life?
You say
Amaj7
G#m7
Amaj7
53
give me time,
and I'll do bet - ter, I swear.
Give me time,
and I'll lead
G#11
A#m
A
B
56
you back to
des - pair,
and I don't want to go back
A#m
A
B
A#m
59
there,
I don't want to go back there,

A
B
A#m
62
I'm nev - er go - ing back to that, and that's a fact ba - by!
A
B
C#m
Amaj7
F#m7
G#m7
64
One of these days you're gon - na bring some home to me,
C#m
Amaj7
F#m7
B
C#m
67
to me.
70
Repeat x4

OUTSIDE

Words and Music by George Michael

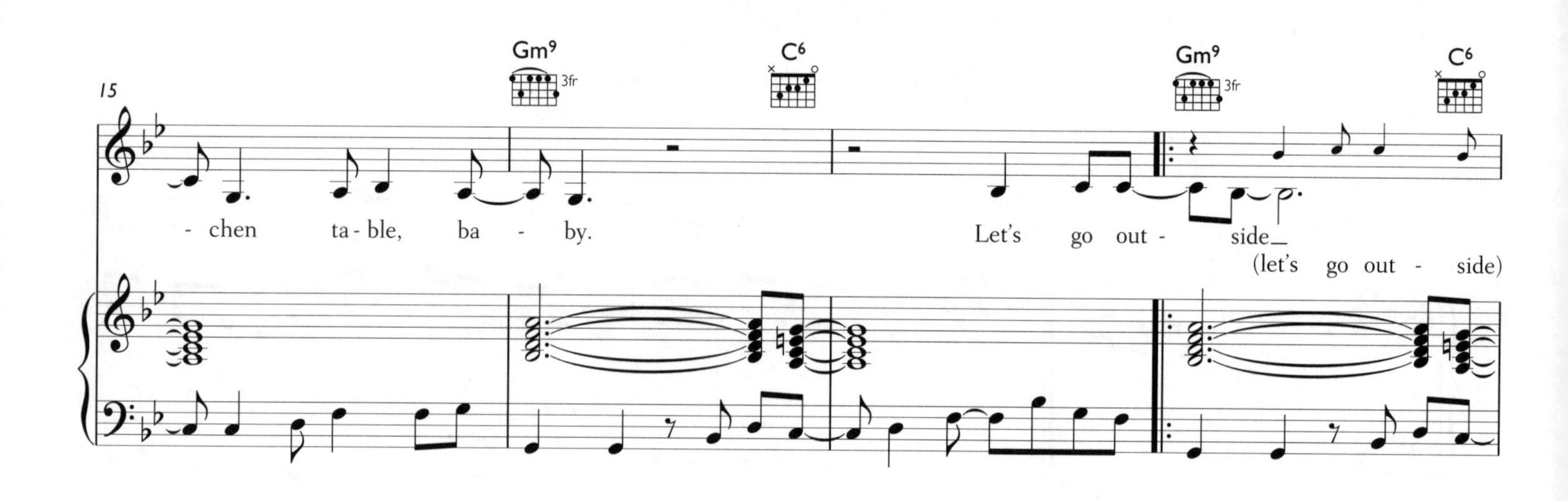
Gm9
3fr
C6
Gm9
3fr
C6
15
- chen ta - ble, ba - by. Let's go out - side
(let's go out - side)

Gm9
3fr
C6
19
in the sun - shine, I know you want to, but you can't say yes,
let's go out -

Gm9
3fr
C6
Gm9
3fr
22
(let's go out - side) in the moon - shine, take me to the pla - ces that I
- side 2° in the mean - time,

1.
C6
Gm9
3fr
C6
25
love best. So my an - gel she says, don't you wor - ry 'bout the things they're say -

Gm9
3fr
C6
Gm9
3fr
C6
28
- ing, yeah, got no friends in high pla - ces and the game that you gave

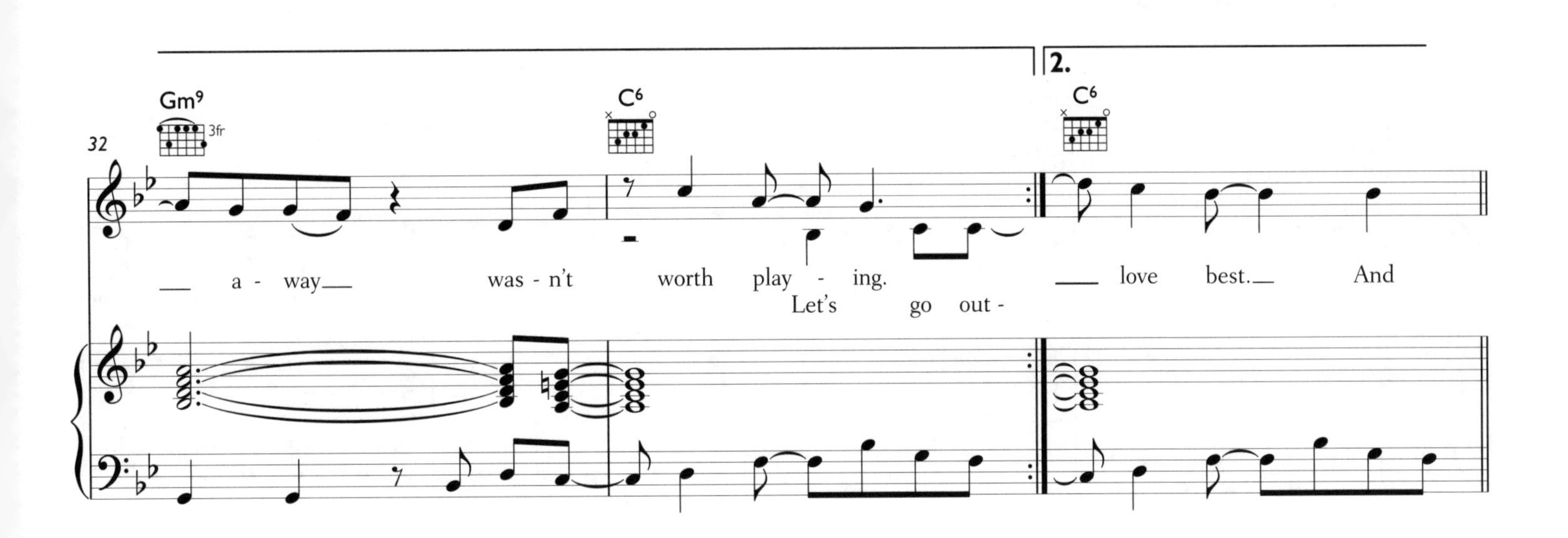
Gm9
3fr
C6
2.
C6
32
a - way was - n't worth play - ing. love best. And
Let's go out -

Cm7 Cm6 Gm9 Gm
yes I've been bad, Doc-tor won't you do with me what you can. You see I
Cm7 Cm6 Gm9
think a-bout it all of the time, twen-ty-four se-ven.
2. I'd ser-vice the com-mu-ni-ty but I
Gm Cm7 Cm6
You say you want it, you got it, I
al-rea-dy have you see! I
ne-ver real-ly said it
Gm9 Gm Cm7 Cm6
be-fore. There's no-thing here but flesh and bone, there's no-thing more,

Dsus4
Gm9
3fr
C6
49
nothing more, there's nothing more.
53
Back to na - ture,
2° Let's go out - side,
just hu - man na -
57
To Coda
- ture.
Get - ting on back to...
Danc - ing on the D - train
I think I'm done with the so -
60
- fa,
I think I'm done with the hall,

Gm9
3fr
C6
63
I think I'm done with the kit - chen ta - ble, ba - by.
66
Let's go out - side
(let's go out - side)
in the sun - shine,
I know you want to, but you
70
can't say yes,
let's go out - side
(let's go out - side)
in the moon - shine,
73
take me to the pla - ces that I love best.
N.C.

G13sus4
76
80
D.𝄋 al Coda
And
𝄌 Coda
Gm9
C6
3fr
83
3
ba - by.
When the moon is high
and the grass is jump-
87
Repeat ad lib. to fade
- in'
come on,
just
keep on
funk - in'.

AS

Words and Music by Stevie Wonder

Bmaj7
Amaj7
7
- buds know to bloom in ear - ly May.
Just as hate
Bmaj7
B7
Emaj7
9
knows love's the cure, you can rest your mind as - sured that I'll
G#m7
A#m11
D#7
G#m7
G#m6
C#m9
F#13
Bmaj7
B9
11
be lov - ing you al - ways.
2. As now can't re - veal the mys - tery of to - mor-
Emaj7
Bmaj7
14
- row, but in pass - ing will grow old - er ev - 'ry - day.

Amaj7
Bmaj7
B9
16
Just as all that's born is new, you know what
Emaj7
G♯m7
A♯m11
D♯7
18
I say is true, that I'll be lov-ing you al - - ways.
G♯m
D♯7/A♯
G♯m/B
C♯7
20
Un-til the rain-bow burns the stars out of the sky. Al - ways.
G♯m
D♯7/A♯
G♯m/B
C♯7
22
Un-til the o - cean co - vers ev - 'ry moun-tain high. Al - ways.

G♯m
D♯7/A♯
G♯m/B
C♯7
4fr
8fr
7fr
4fr
24
Until the day that eight times eight times eight is four. Al -
G♯m
D♯7/A♯
G♯m/B
D♯/F
26
-ways. Until the day that is the day that are no more.
Emaj7
Bmaj7
7fr
Mary J. Blige (female vocals down octave)
28
Did you know that true love asks for no - thing,
Emaj7
Dmaj7
30
her ac-cep-tance is the way we pay.

Emaj7
Bmaj7
Did you know that life has giv - en love a gua - ran - tee to last
C#m7
D#7sus4
D#7
C#m7
F#7
George Michael
through for - ev - er, an - oth - er day.
3. As to - day
4. As a - round
Bmaj7
B9
Emaj7
I know I'm liv - ing but to - mor - row could make me
the sun the earth knows she's re - volv - ing, and the rose
Bmaj7
Amaj7
Mary J. Blige
the past, but that I must - n't fear, 'cause you're here. Now I know
- buds know to bloom in ear - ly May. Now I know

Bmaj7
B9
Emaj7
40
George Michael
deep in my mind the love of me I've left be - hind, and I'll
deep in my mind the love of me I've left be - hind, and I'll
G#m7
4fr
A#m11
6fr
D#7
6fr
G#m
4fr
D#7/A#
8fr
42
Lead vocal ad lib.
be lov - ing you al - ways. Un - til the rain - bow burns the stars
be lov - ing you al - ways. Un - til the day is night and night
G#m/B
7fr
C#7
4fr
G#m
4fr
D#7/A#
8fr
44
out of the sky. Un - til the o - cean co - vers ev -
be - comes the day. Un - til the trees and seas just up
G#m/B
7fr
C#7
4fr
G#m
4fr
D#7/A#
8fr
46
'ry moun - tain high. Un - til the dol - phins fly and par -
and fly a - way. Un - til the day that eight times eight

G#m/B
C#7
G#m
D#7/A#
2° To Coda
48
- rots live at sea.
times eight is four.
Un - til we dream of life and life
Un - til the day that is the day
1.3.
2.
D#/F
D.S al Coda
50
be - comes a dream.
that are no more.
Coda
52
Mary J. Blige
that are no more. Al - ways.
54
Al - ways.
Al - ways.

G♯m
D♯7/A♯
G♯m/B
C♯7
4fr
8fr
7fr
Lead vocal ad lib.
57
Un - til the rain - bow burns the stars out of the sky.
Un - til the day is night and night be - comes the day.
59
Un - til the o - cean co - vers ev - 'ry moun - tain high.
Un - til the trees and seas just up and fly a - way.
61
Un - til the dol - phins fly and par - rots live at sea.
Un - til the day that eight times eight times eight is four.
63
Repeat to fade
Un - til we dream of life and life be - comes a dream.
Un - til the day that is the day that are no more.

FREEEK!

Words and Music by George Michael, Ruadhri Cushnan, Niall Flynn, James Jackman, Stephen Garrett, Timothy Mosley, Kamaal Fareed, James Yancey, Gene Redd, Roy Handy, Cleveland Horne, Robert Bell, Ronald Bell, Robert Mickens, Richard Westfield, Dennis Thomas, George Brown and Claydes Smith

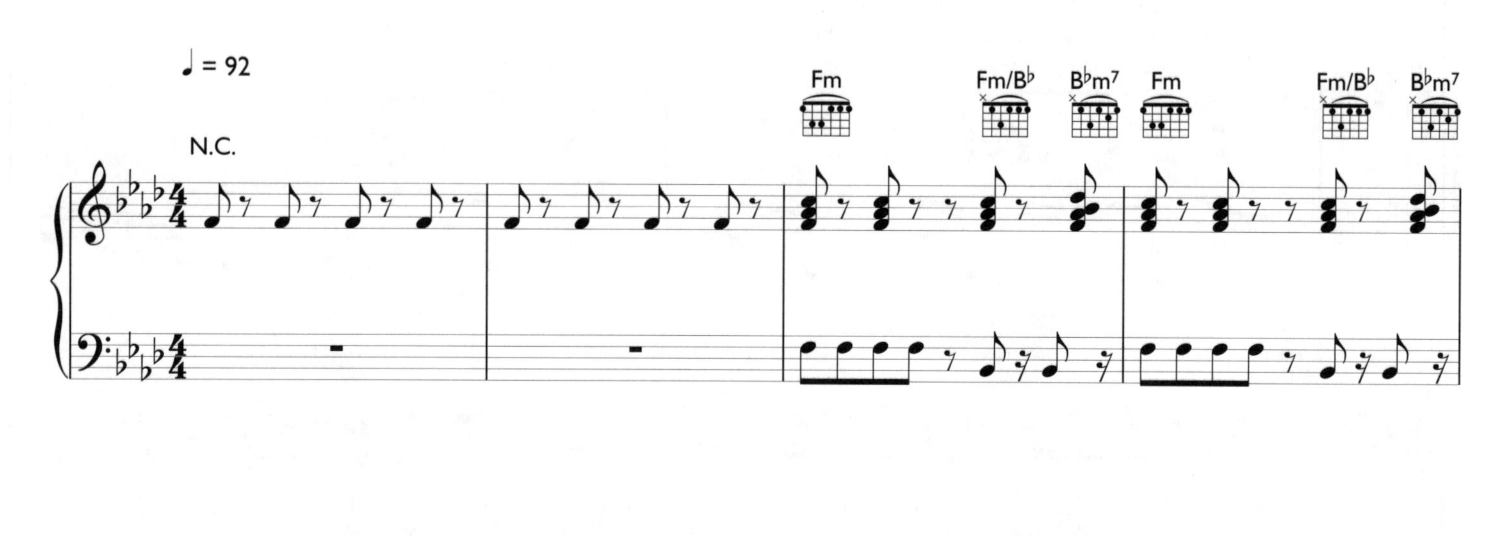

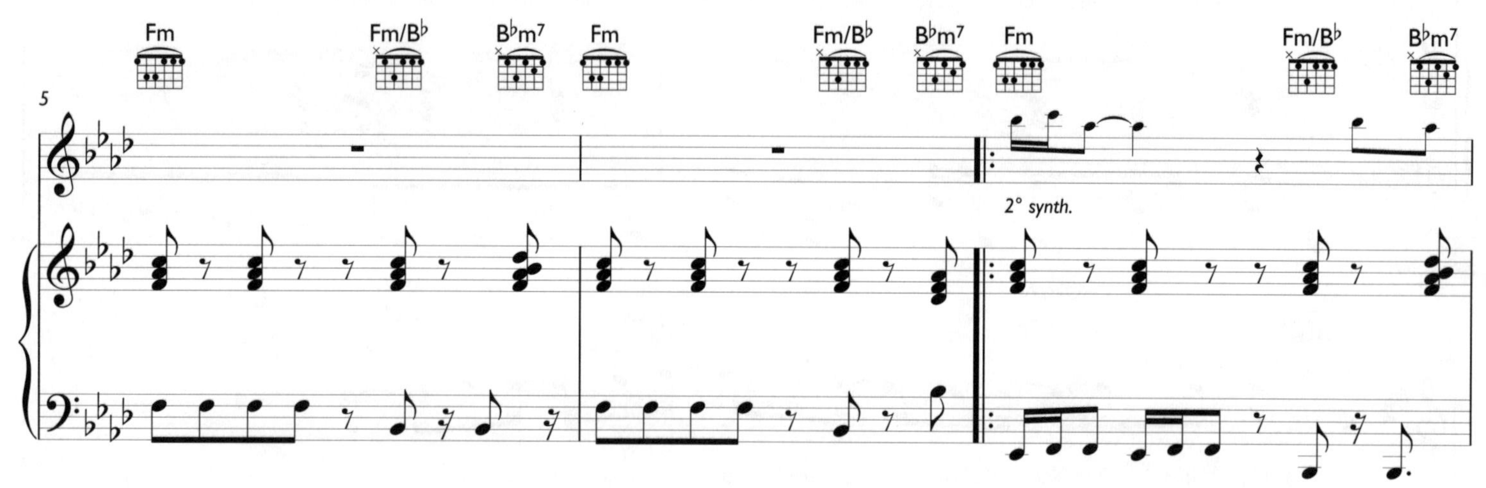

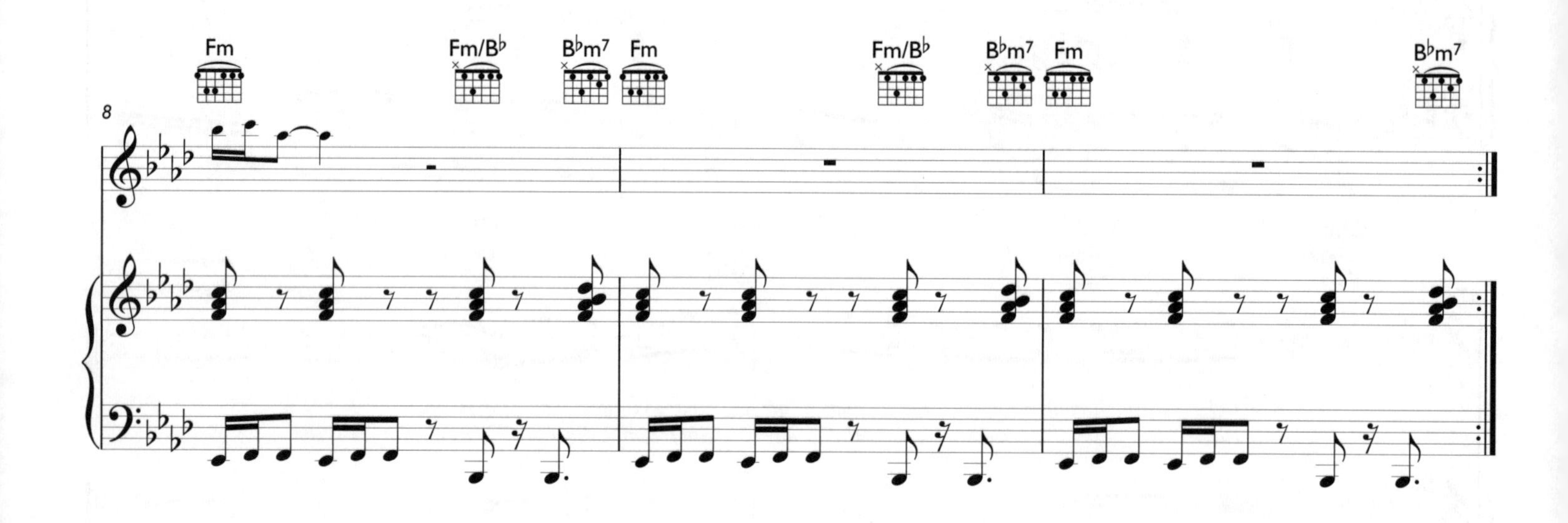

Fm
Fm/B♭
B♭m7
1. You got your - self some ac - tion, said you got your - self a bo - dy.
2. You got your - self some ac - tion, said you got your sex - y Ja - va.
You got your - self an ass with a mind of its own, bring some-thing to the par - ty.
You got your speed con - nec - tion, free chat, f*** that get a lit - tle har - der.
You got your - self ad - dic - ted, you shoot up it saves you time
You got your - self a big bed, you shoot off, take your time
You got your - self a pay - check. I'll be your
(Fa - ces in the pla - ces where the sun don't shine.)
In the house with a bitch and a mouse and your daddy's plastic, how fan - tas - tic yeah.

Fm
Fm/B♭
B♭m7
N.C.
sex - u - al freeek, of the week.
I'll be your in - spi-ra - tion-al bro - ther, yo ma - ma can't you see.
I'll be your sex - u - al freeek, of the week.
I'll be your e - du - ca - tion - al lov - er, your one f*** fan - ta - sy.
Can I come on in my sweet ba - by?
Oh, can I move on in?

Fm
B♭m7
Fm/B♭
30
Oh, can I come on in
my sweet ba - by?
Oh, can I move on in?
33
N.C.
35
Sex - u - al freeek.
37
1.
2.
Sis - ter
I think I need to re - boot - y.
I'll be your

Fm
Fm/B♭
B♭m7
40
sex - u - al freeek, of the week.
I'll be your in - spi-ra - tion-al bro- ther, yo ma-
43
- ma can't you see, I'll be your sex - u - al freeek.
I'll be your
46
e - du-ca - tion-al lov - er, your one f*** fan - ta - sy.
48
Sis - ter.
Sex - u - al freeek.

Fm
B♭m7
Fm
B♭m7
53
said you got your - self a bo - dy. You got your - self an ass with a

Fm
B♭m7
57
and ass world, you got - ta be pre - pared. Come on kids, don't be scared, it's a tits
59
and ass world, you got - ta be pre - pared. Come on kids, you know your
61
mam-ma and your dad - dy don't care. Don't be scared, it's a tits
63
and ass world, you got - ta be pre - pared.
N.C.
Repeat to fade

SHOOT THE DOG

Words and Music by George Michael, Philip Oakey and Ian Burden

17
Dm7
Am7
shoot the dog. It's par-ty time ev'-ry day I spent Sa-tur-day night on
21
Dm7
Am7
No-vo-caine. Called the pigs but no-bo-dy came. I'm gon-na shoot the dog, I'm gon-na
25
Dm7
Am7
shoot the dog. Nine, nine, nine get-ting jig-gy peo-ple did you see that fire in the
29
Dm7
Am7
ci-ty? It's like we're fresh out of de-mo-crat-ic got-ta get your-self a lit-tle some-thing se-mi-

G7sus4
G7
3fr
33
au - to - ma - tic yeah. That's why I'm al-ways get - ting stoned yeah,
37
1.
that's why I'm out there hav-ing fun yeah. Good pup-py, good pup-py roll-ing on o -
41
Dm7
Am7
- ver. 2. Mus - ta - pha, Ma-zel-tov. The Ga - za boys all that
45
ho - ly stuff. I get the feel-ing when it all goes off I'm gon - na shoot the dog, I'm gon - na

Dm7
Am7
49
shoot the dog. So Che-rie my dear could you leave the way clear for sex to-night?
Dm7
Am7
53
Tell him "To-ny, To-ny, To-ny I know that you're hor-ny but there's some-thing 'bout that Bush ain't right"
2.
G7sus4
G7
G7sus4
57
roll-ing on o-ver for The Man
G7
G7sus4
G7
G7sus4
61
The A-ya-toll-ah's get-ting bombed yeah
See Serge-ant Bil-ko hav-ing fun a-gain

G7
G7sus4
G7
65
Good pup - py, good pup - py rolling on o - ver for The Man I be -
F/G
G
F/G
68
- lieve, I be-lieve what the old man said though I know that there's no Lord a - bove I be-lieve in me, I be-lieve in you and you
G
F/G
G
71
know I be-lieve in love. I be - lieve in truth though I lie a lot I feel the pain from push and shove. No
F/G
G
G7sus4
G7
74
mat - ter what you put me through I'll still be - lieve in love, and I say...
3fr

G7sus4
G7
78
Oh yeah Che-rie ba - by, spliff up, spliff up I wan-na
82
kick-back ma-ma and watch the World Cup with you ba - by. The A - ya - toll - ah's get - ting
86
bombed yeah, we're get - ting freak - y to-night yeah, good pup - py, I wan-na
90
kick - back ma - ma and watch the World Cup with you ba - by. Stay with
3fr

G7
G7sus4
3fr
93
me to-night,
let's have some fun while
To - ny's State - side.
It's gon-na be all right
97
(it's gon - na...)
We're gon - na kick - back ma - ma
yeah,
we're get - ting freak - y to - night
100
We're get - ting freak - y.
104
Repeat ad lib. to fade
Good pup - py
I wan-na kick-back ma-ma
yeah,
we're get - ting freak-y to - night...

AMAZING

Words and Music by Jonathan Douglas and George Michael

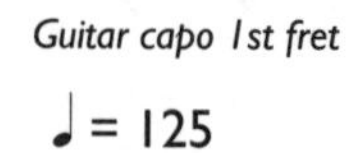

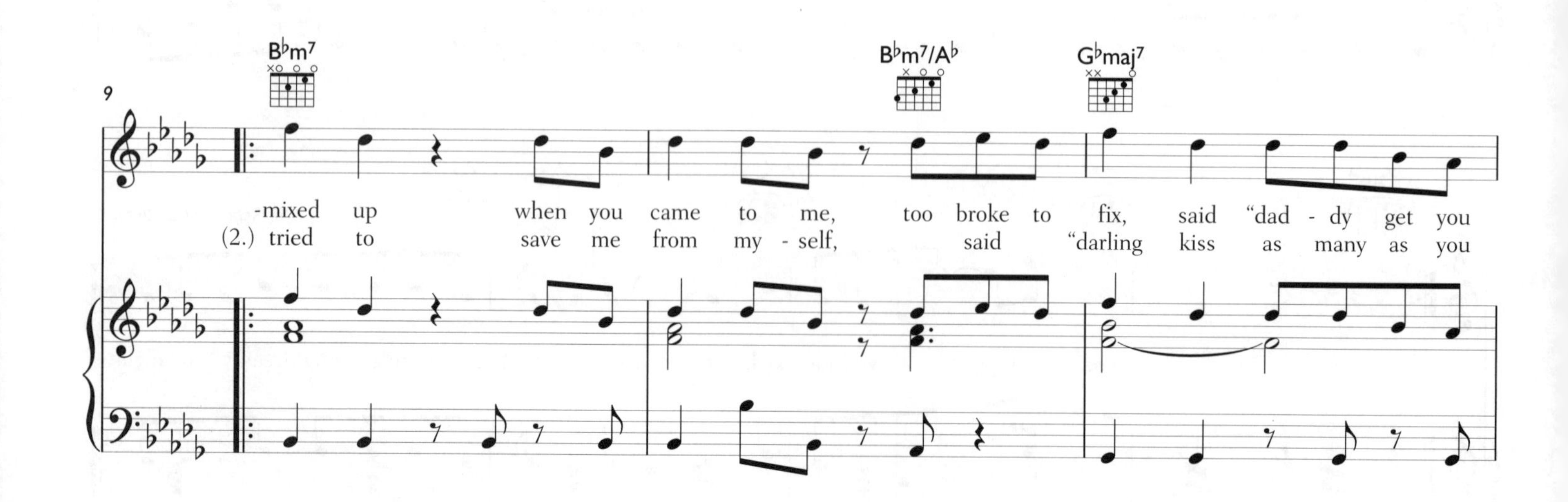

12
G♭maj7/A♭
B♭m7
B♭m7/A♭
gone, I'm mis - sing my ba - by." Still mis - sing my ba -
want! My love's still a - vail - a - ble, and I know you're in -
15
G♭maj7
G♭maj7/A♭
B♭m7
- by... Mmm I was a - stiched up by the
-sa - tia - ble." We're like a - vic - tims of the
18
B♭m7/A♭
G♭maj7
hands of fate, said, how you gon - na make it on your
same dis - ease, look at your big bad dad - dy and your
20
G♭maj7/A♭
B♭m7
B♭m7/A♭
own if luck is a la - dy? Well may - be luck is a la -
mom... And your mom was al - ways act - ing craz -

G♭maj7
E♭m7
23
- dy. I was go - ing down for the third
- y. I was go - ing down for the third
B♭m7
A♭
B♭m7
E♭m7
26
time, my heart was brok - en, I was not o - pen to your sug -
time, my heart was brok - en, I thought that loving you was out of the
G♭maj7
29
- ges - tions. Had so man - y ques - tions that
ques - tion. Then I saw my re - flec - tion, saying
E♭7sus4
B♭m7
B♭m7/A♭
32
Tell me, I guess that Cu - pid was in
you just kissed a - way.
please don't let this go.

G♭maj7
Fm7
35
dis - guise the day you walked in and changed my life.
E♭m7
Fm7
38
I think it's a - maz - ing, the way that love can set
B♭m7
B♭m7/A♭
G♭maj7
41
you free. So now I walk in the mid - day sun, I
Fm7
44
nev - er thought that my sa - viour would come. I think it's a - maz -

1.
E♭m7
E♭m7/D♭
Fm7
B♭m7
47
- ing,
I think it's a - maz - ing.
I think you're a - maz -
(Da, da, da, da, da,
B♭m7/A♭
G♭maj7
G♭maj7/A♭
50
da, da, da, da, da, da, da, da, da, da, da, da, da, da, da, da.)
I think you're a - maz-
53
- ing.
(Da, da, da, da, da, da, da, da, da, da, da, da, da, da, da, da,
2.
56
da, da, da, da, da, da.)
2. You - maz - ing.
(Cel - e - brate the love of the one you're with.)
Cel -

G♭maj7
Fm7
59
- e - brate this life with you ba - by.
(Cel - e - brate the love of the one you're with.) (Cel - e - brate the
E♭m7
Fm7
A♭
62
I think you should cel - e - brate yeah. Don't put your love in chains
love of the one you're with.) (Cel - e - brate the love of the one you're with.)
B♭m7
B♭m7/A♭
G♭maj7
65
ba - by. Now I walk in the mid - day sun, I
(Cel - e - brate the love of the one you're with.) (Cel - e - brate the
Fm7
68
nev - er thought that my sa - viour'd come. I think it's a - maz -
love of the one you're with.) (Cel - e - brate the love of the one you're with.)

E♭m7
Fm7
A♭
B♭m7
71
- ing,
I think you're a - maz - ing. (Da, da, da, da, da,
(Cel - e - brate the love of the one you're with.)
(Cel - e - brate the
B♭m7/A♭
G♭maj7
74
da, da, da, da, da, da, da, da, da, da, da, da, da, da, da, da.)
love of the one you're with.)
(Cel - e - brate the love of the one you're with.)
Fm7
77
(Da, da, da, da, da, da, da, da, da, da,
(Cel - e - brate the love of the one you're with.)
E♭m7
Fm7
A♭
Repeat ad lib. to fade
79
da, da, da, da, da, da, da, da, da, da, da, da.)
(Cel - e - brate the love of the one you're with.)

FLAWLESS (GO TO THE CITY)

Words and Music by George Michael, Paul Alexander,
Nashom Wooden, Oliver Stumm, Eric Matthew and Gary Turnier

B♭maj7
Gmaj7
13
'Cos you're beau - ti - ful...
(perfection)
Beau-ti - ful...
17
(flawless, absolutely flawless)
And it's no good wait - ing by the win - dow, it's no good wait - ing
21
for the sun, please be - lieve me, the things you dream of, they don't fall in the laps of no
25
- one. And it's no good, and it's no good wait - ing wait-

B♭maj7
Gmaj7
29
- ing,
and it's no good,
and it's no good
wait - ing.
33
You got - ta go to the ci - ty,
al - ways the same,
37
al - ways the same
dreams
yeah,
al - ways the same.
Yes you're mov -
41
- ing up.
Well you got - ta think of some - thing
'cos your job
pays you no -

B♭maj7
Gmaj7
45
- thing, but you've got the things God gave you, so the mu - sic may yet be your sa -
49
- viour. Got-ta be some way, some way, got-ta be some way to make your way to the light.
53
1°(all the girls say)
2°(all the boys say)
Got-ta be some way, to - day, to - day, may-be to - night, may-be to - night,
2° they'll see you to - night,
57
and it's al-ways the same.
Al-ways the same.

B♭maj7
Gmaj7
61
Al-ways the same dreams yeah, al-ways the same. Yes you're mo -
1.
B♭maj7
Gmaj7
65
-ving up. You're beau-ti - ful you are, and you know it. Mmm.
B♭maj7
69
You're was - ted here, you're a star in this
Gmaj7
B♭maj7
72
small town of hand-me-downs who don't ev - en know it. Some-times it brings you down

75
Gmaj7
some-times it eats you up, some-times you think that your head's gon-na blow it.
78
B♭maj7
Gmaj7
Does-n't it, does-n't it, does-n't it, does-n't it, does-n't get bet - ter. Don't you know
81
B♭maj7
Gmaj7
you got-ta go to the ci - ty, you got-ta go to the ci - ty, you got-ta reach the oth-er side of the glass
85
B♭maj7
Gmaj7
I think you'll make it in the ci-ty ba - by, I think you know that you are more than just some

2.
B♭maj7
89
fucked piece_ of ass - ing up._ And it's no good_ wait - ing by the win - dow, it's_
Gmaj7
B♭maj7
93
_ no_ good_ wait - ing for the sun. Please be - lieve me, the things you dream of, they don't
Gmaj7
B♭maj7
97
fall in_ the laps of no - one._ And it's no good,_ and it's no good_ wait-
Gmaj7
B♭maj7
101
- ing,_ wait - ing._ And it's no good,_ and it's no good_ wait-

Gmaj7
B♭maj7
105
- ing___ you got-ta go to the ci - ty. 'Cos your job
109
___ pays you no - thing,___ but you've got___ the things___ God gave
112
___ you, so the mu - sic may yet___ be your sa - viour. Do you want a sa - viour, sa -
116
- viour, say,___ say___ that you do.___ Yeah___ you know you're wast - ed___ here,___

Gmaj7
B♭maj7
120
wast - ed here, and there ain't no mir - a - cles
hap-pen-ing an - y-time soon.
124
Al-ways the same,
hap-pen-ing an - y-time soon.
Al-ways the same,
129
al-ways the same,
al-ways the same,
133
Repeat to fade
al-ways the same,
al-ways the same...

AN EASIER AFFAIR

Words and Music by George Michael, Ruadhri Cushnan,
Niall Flynn and Kevin Ambrose

Fmaj7
Cmaj7
17
I told my-self I was straight but I should-n't have wor - ried 'cos my Ma-ker had a bet-ter plan
Dm7
Em7
21
for me, and I'm danc-ing with the freaks now, I'm hav - in', I'm hav - in' so much fun.
Dm7
Em7
Am7
25
What you sow is what you reap now I'll do my dance with ev-'ry - one, been
Dm7
Em7
29
get - ting too much sun, yes, I'm danc - ing with the freaks now, we're hav - in', we're hav - in' too much fun

Dm7
33
Em7
Am7
— for them. Look who's talk-ing guil-ty feet now. Then let me tell you peo-ple it's an
Fmaj7
37
eas - i - er af - fair not liv-ing my life with oth - er peo - ple on my mind,
Em7
41
Dm7
Em7
no, got no - thing to hide from a - ny - one. Yes I'm
Fmaj7
45
walk - ing on new air just liv-ing my life, bet-ter be-lieve I'm gon-na get what's

Em7
Dm7
Em7
49
mine,
see I don't have the time for the ha - ters.
1.
Fmaj7
Cmaj7
53
And all the time that I wast - ed, how care - less of me.
Fmaj7
Cmaj7
57
Too young and stu-pid to see I put my life in their hands.
Fmaj7
Cmaj7
61
Oh, and I know that they want me to hate them, there's no hur - ry, I'll just

65
Dm7
Em7
have to be the big-ger man. And I'm danc-ing with the freaks now, I'm hav - in',
69
Dm7
Em7
I'm ha-vin' so much fun. What you sow is what you reap now I'll
73
Am7
Dm7
Em7
do my dance with ev-'ry-one, been get-ting too much sun. If I turn the oth-er cheek now, we're hav - in',
77
Dm7
Em7
we're ha-vin' too much fun for them. Look who's talk-ing guil-ty feet now Then

2.
Dm7
Em7
Am7
Don't let them tell you who you are is not e - nough,
don't let them tell you that it's wrong, that you won't find love,
don't let them use my life to
put your fut - ure down, don't let them tell you that hap - pi - ness can't be found.
For my life, for my life,

Dm7
Em7
94
take it to the streets there are sto - ries you can keep,
they're just
Am7
Dm7
97
pass - ing you by.
Don't let them tell you who you are is not e - nough,
Em7
Am7
Dm7
100
don't let them tell you that it's wrong, that you won't find love.
Don't let them use my life to
103
Em7
Am7
Repeat and fade
put your fut - ure down,
don't let them tell you that
hap - pi - ness can't be found...

ADDITIONAL © INFORMATION

FASTLOVE

This song contains a sample from "Forget Me Nots" by Rushen, Washington & McFaddin © Baby Fingers Music, Freddie Dee Music & Yamina Music, USA

FREEEK!

Warner/Chappell Music Ltd, London W6 8BS, Warner/Chappell North America Ltd, London W6 8BS, EMI Music Publishing Ltd, London WC2H 0QY, Sony Music Publishing (UK) Ltd, London W1F 7LP, Zomba Music Publishing Ltd, London SW6 1AH, EMI Music Publishing (WP) Ltd, London WC2H 0QY (Publishing) and Music Sales Ltd, London W1T 3LJ (Print) and Universal Music Publishing Ltd, London SW6 4LZ

This song contains samples from "Try Again" by Garrett & Mosley © Herbilicious Music, Black Fountain Music, EMI April Music Inc & WB Music Corp and "Breathe And Stop" by Fareed, Yancey, Redd, Redd, Handy, Horne, Bell, Bell, Mickens, Westfield, Thomas, Brown & Smith © Zomba Music Publishers Ltd, EPHCY Publishing, Polygram International Music Publishing & EMI Longitude Music, USA

SHOOT THE DOG

This song contains a sample from "Love Action" by Oakey & Burden © EMI Virgin Music Ltd & Dinsong Ltd

FLAWLESS (GO TO THE CITY)

This song contains a sample from "Flawless" by Alexander, Wooden, Stumm, Matthew & Turnier © Artificial Music, Eric Matthew Enterprises Inc & Two Twenty Four Music Inc, USA